**BETHANY KEY**

# HOW TO ANALYZE PEOPLE WITH DARK PSYCHOLOGY

A SPIDE GUIDE TO READING HUMAN PERSONALITY TYPES BY ANALYZING BODY LANGUAGE

## © Copyright 2021 - All rights reserved.

The content contained within this book may not be reproduced, duplicated or transmitted without direct written permission from the author or the publisher. Under no circumstances will any blame or legal responsibility be held against the publisher, or author, for any damages, reparation, or monetary loss due to the information contained within this book. Either directly or indirectly.

**Legal Notice:** This book is copyright protected. This book is only for personal use. You cannot amend, distribute, sell, use, quote or paraphrase any part, or the content within this book, without the consent of the author or publisher.

**Disclaimer Notice:** Please note the information contained within this document is for educational and entertainment purposes only. All effort has been executed to present accurate, up to date, and reliable, complete information. No warranties of any kind are declared or implied. Readers acknowledge that the author is not engaging in the rendering of legal, financial, medical or professional advice. The content within this book has been derived from various sources. Please consult a licensed professional before attempting any techniques outlined in this book.

By reading this document, the reader agrees that under no circumstances is the author responsible for any losses, direct or indirect, which are incurred as a result of the use of information contained within this document, including, but not limited to, errors, omissions, or inaccuracies.

# TABLE OF CONTENTS

**HOW TO ANALYZE PEOPLE WITH DARK PSYCHOLOGY** ............ 0

**INTRODUCTION** ............ 3

**CHAPTER 1: MIND CONTROL** ............ 6
- Mind Control ............ 6
- Positive Forms of Mind Control ............ 9
- Common Techniques of Mind Control ............ 10
- Some of the Tricks to Use for You to Control Your Interlocutors ............ 12

**CHAPTER 2: TYPES OF MIND CONTROL** ............ 16
- Brainwashing ............ 17
- Hypnosis ............ 19
- Manipulation ............ 22
- Persuasion ............ 23
- Deception ............ 24

**CHAPTER 3: HOW TO READ PEOPLE** ............ 26
- Facial Expressions ............ 26
- Hands, Arms, and Gestures ............ 28
- Body Posture and Movement ............ 30
- Reading Lies in People ............ 31

**CHAPTER 4: USERS OF DARK PSYCHOLOGY** ............ 36
- Who Uses Dark Psychology These Days? ............ 36
- The Triad of Dark Psychology ............ 37
- The Manipulator ............ 39
- A Sadist ............ 40
- The manipulator in a relationship ............ 40

**CHAPTER 5: BEHAVIORS EXHIBITED BY ATTACKERS** ............ 44
- Emotional Intelligence and Manipulation ............ 44
- Characteristics of Manipulators ............ 48

**CONCLUSION** ............ 64

# Introduction

Every aspect of human life has two sides-positive and negative, but it depends on the human how he or she utilizes it for their good as well as for others. Consider manipulation as a part of dark psychology, and it is used greatly for the wrongdoings and harmful deeds. On the other hand, it can be utilized positively as well, but it's all in your hand how you want to utilize it. As far as persuasion is concerned, people use it in every field and part of life. For example, a salesman will always try to persuade you to buy his or her recommended product even if you do not want to. Persuasion also has two aspects of being applied. If you try to persuade a person to do something illegal or unethical, that is part of dark psychology but if you persuade someone to get out or leave a certain thing that is not beneficial in any means, let's say suicide, then you are using it for the purpose of good. Everything you do or perceive is totally in the human mind, and you are the controller of it. If you don't want to, then no one can make you do things without your will and consent. Also, it is an essential part of living life to observe your surroundings and the people who are around you. If you do not notice the small things and interpret them wisely, then you are more likely to fall prey for something negative and hazardous. Facial expressions, body language, gestures, and the words and tone used, can predict a lot about people if observed closely. If you fail to recognize such signals that are inclined towards negativity, then you will be unable to keep yourself safe from them. Dark psychology is considered to start from the point where you have no intent or motive to do things except for your self-satisfaction and pleasure, and in return, it is damaging to the other person or even the community. Every living individual has this dark side, but not all of them let that side overcome them. Once you are exposed to that side, there is no coming back. So always watch yourself and your surroundings so that you can keep yourself off of any harm. Persuasion, manipulation, and other forms of influence are ubiquitous. You can pick up on some obvious signs here and there, but there are also hidden secret ways that others control you which you might never be able to fully comprehend.

To those who aren't fully aware of manipulation and what it is all about, it is hard to see that this process takes up three steps. Most of us will just think of manipulation as one thing—there needs to be two things in addition to the act of manipulation, which will make sure that the manipulation is successful. Perhaps you are trying to sell something, maybe yourself or your brand, and you need to figure out how to get people to be more persuaded by you to help you achieve the things that you want in this life. No matter where you are or what you are trying to do, you have all the tools that you will ever need to be persuasive or influential with you already.

Before getting into this book, there are a few things that you need to know to be introduced to this topic to get into the right mindset as you read through this text. First, understand that there are no two manipulators that are alike. There are no two easily persuaded people that are the same either. Though it might seem like this sometimes, especially since you can influence a group all at once, you can't let yourself fall into a thinking pattern where you place everyone in the same category.

Don't blame yourself for not being aware of the ways that you have been manipulated in the past. Regret isn't going to do you any

# Chapter 1:

# Mind Control

## MIND CONTROL

Mind control is a term that is used for several psychological phenomena such as mind control, coercive control, brainwashing, coercive persuasion, malignant use of group dynamics, and a lot more. It is a psychological theory with many names. The many names given to the theory are a clear indication of the fact that there is a lack of agreement that makes room for distortion and confusion, especially in the hands of those that intend to make use of it covertly for their selfish interests.

One can, however, agree with the fact that mind control easily falls under the umbrella of influence and persuasion which deals with the way people change other people's beliefs and behaviors. While some would like to argue that all falls under manipulation, it is important to take note of the missing distinctions in this argument.

It is much better to think of influence as a continuum because at one end there are the ethical and respectful influences that make room for giving respect to an individual concerning his or her rights while at the other end there are destructive influences that rip off a person's independence, identity and his ability to come up with critical and logical thoughts.

When it comes to the darker side of the continuum, we talk about cults and sects. These are the groups of people who make use of deception and mind control skills in taking advantage of its member's strengths and weaknesses to satisfy the selfish desires of the cult leaders.

There are one-on-one cults which are intimate relationships where a person manipulates and exploits others using their influence. These are cultic relationships which are a smaller version of the larger groups that may prove to be destructive as a result of the fact that all the time and attention available are directed towards a person. These relationships may come in the form of husband/wife, pastor/worshipper, teacher/student, or therapist/client.

The best way to pin a definition to mind control is to look at it from the angle of a system of certain influences that can disrupt a person at their core and at their identity level which has to do with their preferences, beliefs, behaviors, relationships, decisions and so on.

Mind control creates a new pseudo-identity or pseudo-personality for the person and can be used in several ways to the benefit of others or that of the person himself. For example, mind control can be used for the benefit of addicts while it can also be used in bad or unethical ways.

This practice is not uncommon as it is not a mystery or dark art that is known to only a select few. It is merely a combination of words and group pressures that are packaged in a way that makes room for the manipulator to create a sense of dependence on his followers. This helps the followers make personal decisions while thinking that they are independent beings who are free to decide on their own.

When a person becomes a victim of mind control, he is unaware of the influence process as well as the changes that are taking place within him.

In discussing this topic, however, it is of utmost importance to take note of certain distinctions, as some points need to be made clear.

First, mind control is a subtle but very insidious process which means that the individual is largely unaware of the grave effects of the influence that is being imposed on them. This is the reason why they typically make little change over time with the belief that they are making decisions for themselves, when all the decisions that they are making are made for them.

It is insidious because the purpose of mind control in some cases is to entrap and cause harm to the victim.

Another distinct point to note is that it is a process that doesn't just happen in an instant. It usually takes a lot of time, which depends on factors like the skills of the manipulator, the methods that the manipulator has decided to make use of, the length of time that the victim was exposed to the techniques, and other personal factors.

However, these days manipulators do not require a whole year or several months as they have become sufficiently skilled in such a way that they can control a person's mind within a few hours.

Also, there is usually force involved in controlling the minds of others. This may not come in the form of physical force but there is certainly some form of psychological and social force/pressure.

The main aim to control the thoughts of the person you are interacting with is to achieve your desired intention. You will get many things if you can take control of the other person's mind. The approach and the techniques to use will determine whether you will be successful in achieving your goal.

You need to get hold of their unconscious to influence them. Train to be a master in controlling and at times manipulating your partner's mind and thoughts. It is attainable to take control of the intention of someone. You need to apply some techniques, and you will succeed.

## POSITIVE FORMS OF MIND CONTROL

When used the right way, mind control techniques can make a substantial change in your life for the better. Mind control can teach you how to do this:

### REMAIN IN CHECK

If you'd let your mind wander freely, who knows where it might lead you. One of the most distracting and dangerous thoughts is that everyone tends to be leading us down a dark and negative path. Without mind control to compel you to take over and drive your thoughts in the direction you want them to go, the concentration you need to remain on top of your game may be difficult to sustain.

## PROTECT YOURSELF

With proper mental control training, you can teach yourself how to become more resilient and protect yourself from the manipulator's willful ways. Mind control will improve and reaffirm your self-confidence by reminding you that you are a strong, positive, and capable person, and no one will ever make you doubt your abilities.

## COMMON TECHNIQUES OF MIND CONTROL

There are different ways which people use to control the minds of others, below are some of these techniques:

### SUBLIMINAL MESSAGING:

These are either visual or auditory messages that are sent to a receiver's brains to bypass the person's normal conscious perceptions. To do this effectively, the mind controller flashes these messages to the other person's brain without giving the person's eyes the chance to capture/see the image or by making sounds inaudible for the receiver's ears.

The messages are sent directly to the brain. The mind controller aims to influence the other person and they do that effectively with the use of this technique.

### BRAINWAVE SYNCHRONIZATION:

For everything a person does or thinks, there is a league of neurons that communicate with each other in the brain. These neurons generate and transmit electrical signals between themselves, creating patterns that are in the form of waves, which are known as brainwaves. For different states of mind of a person, there are different resultant frequencies of these brainwaves.

Thus, the question becomes whether it is possible to get to a predetermined state of the mind.

## Neurolinguistic Programming (NLP):

This is a technique that has its basis in the idea that successful behavioral patterns can be made possible in either the self or other people through the modification of underlying thought patterns as well as interpersonal relationships or interactions.

## Cognitive Behavioral Therapy:

This is a therapeutic technique that may not be related to mind control, but it works perfectly when it comes to the underlying principle of the modification of a person's behavior, known as behavioral modification, based on corresponding thought modification.

## Hypnosis:

This is a mind-control tool that is used by professional hypnotists to fish out a person's suggestible subconscious mind by moving past the conscious and analytical mind to create positive thoughts or replace old negative beliefs that the mind has held onto for a long time.

People in sports have used hypnosis successfully. It has also been used in other fields like education, therapy, as well as self-improvement to boost a person's self-confidence and get rid of phobias, fears, and bad habits. It is used for relaxation and stress relief too.

According to the National Institute of Health, hypnosis is an effective tool in the reduction of some kinds of pains which include the pain from cancer. Also, hypnosis has been proven to have some self-help benefits. It has been said to be a useful tool in any attempt to change the thought process of another person for things like persuasion, negotiation, or sales.

When hypnosis is used in this manner, it is known as conversational hypnosis which is based on the techniques created/developed by the

American psychiatrist and medical hypnotherapist Milton H. Erickson.

## SOME OF THE TRICKS TO USE FOR YOU TO CONTROL YOUR INTERLOCUTORS

### PAY ATTENTION

Pay attention to your interlocutor, and they will have the confidence to express what they feel. That will make them pour out their heart to you, and you will have a base to get control of their mind in any direction that you want.

When you get them to trust you, they will not keep anything from you. You will have the entire picture, and you will know how to approach them.

### MAKE SURE YOU TALK ABOUT WHAT MAKES THEM HAPPY AND WHAT SEEMS TO INTEREST THEM

If you get into a topic and you may not be conversant about the issue, ask questions as a way to show that you are interested. Showing that the talk is interesting to you will earn you more trust. You should tolerate them even if the conversation is boring. That way, you will be in a position to control their minds. Being attentive is a way of showing friendliness, and that will mean pleasant conversation.

### HYPNOTISM

It is a great approach to take control of someone's mind when used in the right way. When used correctly, it will help you put your interlocutor in a trance within the first few minutes of your conversation. It is a way of seducing them, and you will get them to act on your suggestions.

## CONTROL THE GUARD

To make any progress in mind-controlling, you need to suppress the brain shield. It is the conscious mind that you need to deal within the first place. Use softer as well as subtle techniques to make sure that your interlocutor has relaxed.

Try and get them to be in your debt, and this will prove influential. It is okay if you perform favors for your interlocutor to make it simpler to control them. Doing them good from time to time will make them feel an obligation to do good in return. Doing all this will give you a better position in the way you relate. It is advantageous to do this regularly, and it will raise the perception of superiority. The superiority will allow you to access more things that are in the interlocutor's mind. You will have more power since the feeling of guilt in the other person's mind will turn them to your will quickly.

## BE GOOD TO THEM

Be kind and offer multiple choices to them. There being overwhelming choices, their imagination will persuade them to try nearly all of them. Try and show them that following your idea would be the best thing for them to do. That will make them do what you want, and that will be an assurance that you already have control over their mind. Let what they imagine take over to leading them to see how your suggestion is powerful. Use imagination to find the best that you can acquire from a person.

## REPEAT SOMETHING OVER AND OVER AGAIN

Repeating something many times makes it sturdy, and that means that what we perceive is what we believe to be real. If something happens several times, your interlocutor's mind will register that as being the real thing. Repetition is known to be a vital tool in helping people control the brain as well as the thoughts of others. To solidify a concept in someone's mind, you need to repeat it as many times as possible. Use the repetition approach to your advantage, and you will have access to someone's brain without them having a clue of it.

## PRACTICE BEING POSITIVE

Make your ideas look as high as possible and demonstrate how they will end up achieving success. The positive technique makes you look supportive, even when you may not be. Engage in positive interaction, and no should not be an answer. A negative reply can act as a powerful distraction, and it will not give you the ability to control the other person's thoughts. Give yes for an answer even if you know that the results will be negative. That will make the people around you think that you are supportive as well as thoughtful. Spinning things toward the possible will lead you in achieving your desired results without the other person knowing that you are controlling their mind.

## MAINTAIN A HARMONIOUS RELATIONSHIP

Going directly to the exact thing that you want them to do will trigger their curiosity and make them think critically. If they get active in thinking, your entire plan to control their mind may go into ruin. You will have lost your control over them which is not your primary aim. Use the best suitable methods to strengthen the link and make sure that your interlocutor trusts you. When they believe you, they will have no difficulty in putting their confidence in you.

## SEEK TO KNOW WHAT MOTIVATES THEM

Pay full attention to what they have to say, and it will be appropriate if you watch their nonverbal response. You not only need to focus on what motivates them but look into the most powerful motivator. Their most crucial motivator will give a clue on how you need to put your point across. Manipulating this motivator will be the easiest as well as the best strategy to help you in controlling their minds. What they give the most value when it comes to decision making will be of great importance. Try and remember the steps that they have used before to make decisions and try to manipulate them.

## CREATE CONFIDENCE

You must let your interlocutor view themselves as being the hero. It serves as an excellent way to convince them to do what you want without them noticing you have taken control. Demonstrate to your interlocutor their perception matters in your context. When you achieve having their confidence, you will address anything to them with a lot of ease. Tell them how important it would be for them to be directly involved in your ideas. You need to tell them that they will own the credit once the ideas become successful.

## MAKE USE OF THEIR EMOTIONS

There is an approach that you can apply to how somebody feels so that you can control them. When someone has mixed feelings, they may not know that they are monitoring them. They will do what you want to be propelled by what they feel.

You can use a situation that you know has addicted your interlocutor to make them do what you desire. Anger can also be an excellent weapon to take control of someone. Use a wise way that will not alarm them of your aim to induce irritation in your interlocutor.

# Chapter 2:

# Types of Mind Control

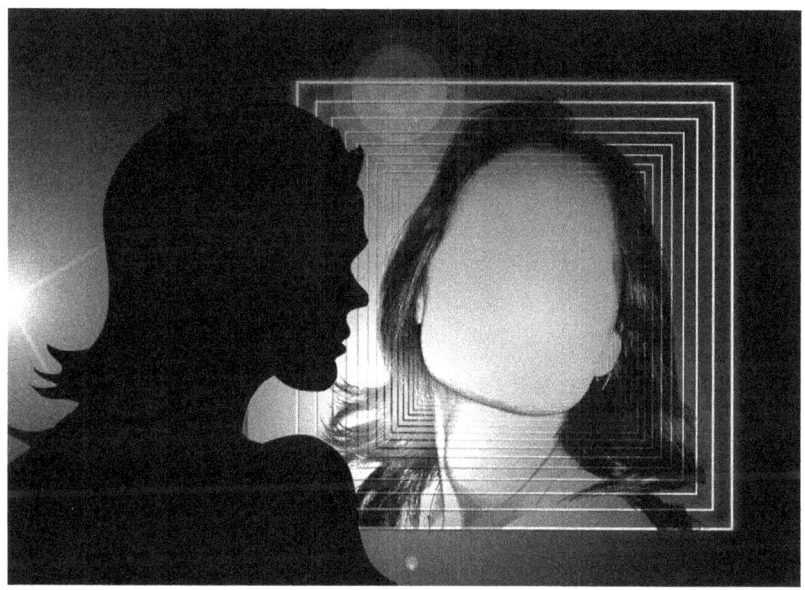

For several years now, the theory of mind control has been about. People were both fascinated and afraid of what would happen if someone could control their minds and make them do things contrary to their will. There are countless conspiracy theories about government leaders and other influential individuals who use their abilities to monitor what small groups of people do. Even some court cases were brought up using the brainwashing excuse as an explanation of why they committed the crime they are accused of. Despite the play-up of mental control depicted in the media and films, little is understood about the various forms of mental control and how each of them functions.

Although many different types of mind control can be used to control the intended victim, the most commonly thought of are five. This involves hypnosis, brainwashing, coercion, persuasion, and deceit. These are all to be discussed in the following.

# BRAINWASHING

Brainwashing is the first kind of mind control to be debated. Brainwashing is essentially the process where someone would be convinced to give up convictions they had in the past and take on new principles and ideals. There are many ways this can be achieved, but not all of them are considered evil.

For instance, if you're from an African nation and then moving to America, you are always forced to change your beliefs and principles to fit in with the new community and climate in which you live. On the other hand, people in concentration camps, or when a new dictatorial regime takes over, will also go through the process of brainwashing to convince citizens to obey in peace. Many people misunderstand what brainwashing is about. Many people have more cynical ideas about the procedure, like mind-control systems that are funded by the government and thought to be quickly turned on with a remote control. On the other side of things, some skeptics don't believe brainwashing is possible at all, and whoever says it is has spread lies. The form of brainwashing will probably fall somewhere between these two theories.

During the brainwashing practice, the target can be convinced by a mixture of techniques to change their views about something. In this method, there is not just one technique that can be used, and it can be difficult to bring the practice into a tidy little package. The subject will also be disconnected from all the things they learn. From there, they are broken down into an emotional state which makes them fragile before new concepts are implemented. As this new knowledge is absorbed by the subject, they will be rewarded for sharing ideas and thoughts that go with these new ideas. This should be used to justify the brainwashing that is taking place is rewarding.

Brainwashing is nothing new to society. For a long time, people have been using such techniques. For example, those who were prisoners of war were sometimes broken down in a historical context, before being convinced to change sides. Some of those most successful cases would result in the inmate becoming a very fervent convert to the new side. In the beginning, such activities were very new and would always be applied based on who was in command. The concept of brainwashing was developed over time, and a few more methods were added to make the practice more widespread. The newer techniques will focus on the field of psychology because many of those concepts were used to show how people, by persuasion, could change their minds.

Several steps go along with the process of brainwashing. It's not something that can happen to you just as you walk down the street and talk to someone you just met. First of all, one of the main demands that come with successful brainwashing is that the subject should be kept in isolation. If the subject is around other people and experiences, they can learn how to behave like an adult, and there will be no brainwashing at all.

They can undergo a process designed to break down their selves if the subject is isolated. They're told all the facts they know are wrong, and they're made to feel like they're wrong with everything they do. The subject will feel like they're bad after months of going through all of this and will be overwhelmed by the guilt. Once they have reached this point, the manipulator will begin to lead them to the desired new system of beliefs and identity. The subject would be led to believe that all of the new opinions are their own, and therefore, they are more likely to last. The entire brainwashing cycle can take months or even years or complete. It's not something that's going to happen in just a conversation, and it won't be able to happen outside of detention camps and a few isolated situations for the most part.

For the most part, when someone is simply trying to convince others of a different point of view, those are people who experience brainwashing. For example, if you're in an argument with a friend, and they're telling you their ideas make sense, you've technically been through brainwashing. Sure, it may not be bad, and you might objectively think about it all, but you were also persuaded to alter previously held convictions. It is unlikely that someone undergoes real brainwashing where they would have changed their whole belief system. It will usually occur during the process of getting around to a new point of view, irrespective of whether or not the tactics used were forceful.

# HYPNOSIS

The next, well-known form of mind control is hypnosis. The several meanings of what hypnosis is are different. Hypnosis is a mutual activity, according to the American Psychological Association, in which the hypnotist will provide suggestions that the patient will respond to. Many people have become familiar with hypnosis techniques thanks to popular performances in which participants are told to perform ridiculous or unusual tasks. Another form of hypnosis that is gaining in popularity is the type that uses this practice for its therapeutic and medical advantages, especially when it comes to reducing anxiety and pain. In some cases, hypnosis has been able to reduce dementia symptoms in a few patients. There are, as you can see, several different explanations that can be used for hypnosis. If the hypnotist will give solutions that may be detrimental or alter the way the client behaves in their situation, that is the point where it starts to become mind control.

When most people hear about hypnosis, they think of a person on stage who swings a watch back and forth to put the participant in a trance. If you go to a stage show for amusement, you might picture some of the absurd actions performed by the participants in your mind. Those who are going through what is considered to be real hypnosis are going through a very different process. "The individual is not hypnotized by the hypnotist. The hypnotist then acts as a sort of coach or mentor whose task is to help the person become hypnotized, "John Kihlstrom said. This means the hypnotist is trying to bring the client into a relaxed state of mind, so they are more open to suggestions offered.

Most of the hypnosis sufferers claim they are in a kind of sleeplike dream state. Notwithstanding these feelings, while the patient is in a state under hypnosis, it includes vivid hallucinations, increased suggestibility, and concentrated attention. This new condition makes them more responsive to suggestions offered by the hypnotist. The effects that hypnosis can have on subjects are difficult to describe, since the experiences can differ quite a bit for each person who undergoes it. Some participants will describe the feeling as though they are disconnected from the whole process, some will feel highly comfortable during the hypnosis, and others will even believe like their acts will take place beyond their conscious choices. On the other hand, individuals will claim to be fully aware of their surroundings and will even be able to conduct conversations during their hypnotic state.

Several studies done by Ernest Hilgard show that hypnosis can be used to alter the beliefs of the subject. Hilgard's experiment included a warning to the subject that they should not experience any pain in their head. The subject had their arm stuck in some ice water after they were told this. Those who did this experiment and did not get hypnotized had to take their arms out of the water in just a few seconds because they felt pain. Many who had been hypnotized could leave their arms in the water without experiencing any pain for a few minutes. Though more research is required, this study shows how powerful mind control can be when using the technique of hypnosis.

There are several different uses of hypnosis illustrated by studies that include:

Treatment of chronic pain like the one associated with rheumatoid arthritis. Treatment and avoidance of the suffering that comes from childbirth.

Reducing the symptoms related to dementia.

Since using hypnotherapy, some ADHD patients have reported a reduction in their symptoms.

To reduce cases of vomiting and nausea in patients going through chemotherapy.

Pain control during a dental procedure. Eliminating and reducing skin disorders, such as psoriasis and warts, alleviating symptoms linked to Irritable Bowel Syndrome.

These are only a few of the uses for which hypnosis has become popular. While many people believe that using hypnosis is used to manipulate the subject and make it perform cruel actions or reject their values, the most popular applications are those to enhance individuals' safety.

Most experts believe that hypnosis as a method of mind control is not a fact. Although it may be possible to convince the mind to make a few changes in the subject's behavior, it is impossible that the subject will change their whole belief system even by this process. Many of the people who are trained in this field would use it to assist the subject in handling self-improvement and discomfort rather than attempting to take over their minds.

# MANIPULATION

Manipulation is another type of mind control which can be used in various ways to decide how the person thinks. Manipulation is referred to in this guidebook as psychological manipulation. It is a sort of social power that serves to alter other people's actions or understanding. It is done using methods that are hostile, insulting, and underhanded. This form of mind control is used, often to the detriment of others, to advance the one controlling desires. The approaches employed are also perceived as manipulative, devious, coercive, and exploitative. Most people can understand when controlled or others controlled around them, but they don't identify that as a form of mind control. It can also be a difficult form of mind control to resist as the coercion generally takes place between the subject and someone they know well. Manipulation leaves the subject feeling as if they have no choice. They would have been fed lies or half-truths outright, and they would not know the full severity of the case until it was too late. When they find out ahead of time about the situation, the manipulator would be able to threaten and use the subject to achieve the final target. By fact, the subject gets lost, and the manipulator will have worked it out in such a way that they won't fall into trouble, the subject will take the blame or get hurt when it comes to it, and the manipulator can make it to their final target.

The worst thing about this is that the manipulator is unable to sense their subject's needs or any other person's needs; they won't know whether the subject gets harmed in the process and if it's emotional or physical damage. Although the subject will be involved emotionally in the situation, the manipulator will be able to walk away (as long as they achieve their ultimate goal) without feeling any guilt or regret for what happened along the way. This can be a dangerous type of mind control because the manipulator will be an expert at it, capable of blackmailing, threatening, and doing whatever else is needed; often, they will even be able to turn it around, so the target feels like they're going insane.

# PERSUASION

Persuasion is another type of mind controlthatacts to manipulate the subject's actions, emotions, thoughts, attitudes, and beliefs. There are many different reasons why persuasion could be used in everyday life, and it's often a necessary form of communication to get people on the same page with different ideas. For business, for example, the persuasion mechanism can be used to shift the attitude of a person about anything, such as, a concept, or event that is happening. During the process, either written or spoken words are used to pass reasoning, feelings, or information on to the other person. Convincing another may be used to satisfy a personal gain. This may include encouraging trials, when delivering a sales pitch, or during an election campaign. Although none of these are considered negative or bad, they are all used to convince the listener to act or think in some way. One definition of persuasion is that one uses their own personal or professional power to alter others' attitudes or behaviors. There are also many different forms of persuasion known; the process of changing beliefs or attitudes by appealing to reason and reasoning is known as systemic persuasion; the process of changing beliefs and attitudes by appealing to feelings or behaviors is known as heuristic persuasion.

Persuasion is a form of control of the mind that is used all the time in society. When you talk about politics to someone, you can try to convince them to think the same way you do. If you listen to a political advertisement, you are motivated to vote in one direction or another. If anyone wants to sell you a new product, there's a lot of persuasion going on there. This form of mind control is so widespread that most people don't even know it's happening to them. The problem will occur when someone takes the time to convince you to believe in beliefs and principles that do not suit your belief system. There are several different kinds of persuasion on sale. Maybe all of them have negative intent, but they will all try to get the target to change their minds about something. When a political candidate appears on television on election day, they try to get the subject, or the voter, to vote on the ballot a certain way. The company that produced the advertising is trying to get the audience to purchase that product when you see a commercial on television or online. These are all forms of persuasion bent on trying to get the target to change the way they think.

## DECEPTION

Finally, deception is often considered a form of mind control because of its potential effect on the subject. Deception is used to spread assumptions about events and things in the subject's life which are not real, regardless of whether they are full lies or just partial lies. Deception may include several different items like hand sleight, concealment, disguise, and diversion. This kind of mind control is dangerous because the subject sometimes does not know that there is any kind of mind control at all. We are persuaded that when the complete opposite is right, one thing is real. It can become dangerous when the deception hides details that would keep the subject secure. Often during relationships, deception is seen and will usually lead to feelings of distrust and betrayal between the two partners. There has been a violation of the relationship rules when deceit happens, and it may make it impossible for the partner to trust the other for a long time. It can be particularly dangerous because most people are used to trusting those around them, especially partners and friends, and often expect them to be true to them. When they find out they're being misled by someone they're close to, they may have problems with trusting people, and they won't have the sense of security they're used to.

Deception can trigger several problems in a relationship, or the manipulator and subject. Once they find out about the deception, the subject will have a lot of issues trusting the manipulator in the future. There will be occasions where the lie is made to help the partnership out. This may involve things like not asking a partner when someone says they mean something. Other times the deception is of a more spiteful or harmful nature, such as when the manipulator hides important information from the subject or even deceives the person as to who they are. All people believe that deceit is unethical and should not be performed, no matter what form of deceit is deployed.

# Chapter 3:

# How to Read People

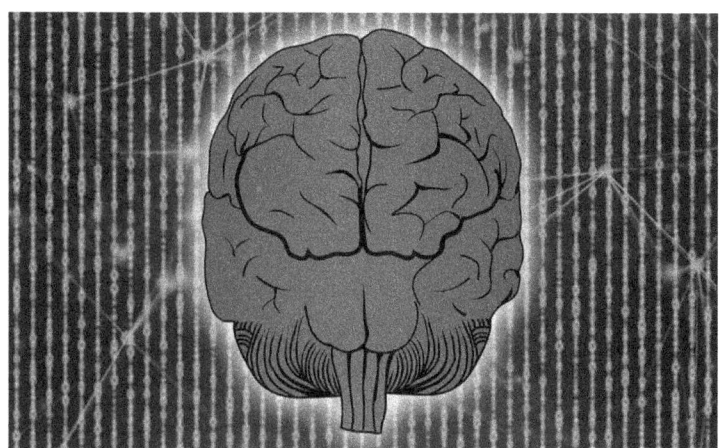

What you say communicates only half of what people hear. 40-50% of the message you send comes from your body language. Since the last century, we have made a lot of progress in understanding the thousands of non-verbal communication meanings. Here are some of the most important findings:

## FACIAL EXPRESSIONS

How good are you at reading facial expressions? There are currently online tests that tell you whether you're good at reading facial expressions or not. Some tests like Reading the Mind in the Eyes Test checks to see whether you can read a person's mind simply by looking at their eyes. If you're interested in taking the test yourself, check the website: socialintelligence.labinthewild.org/mite. See how well you fare and then just come back to this book if you want. For purposes of improving communication, we're going to include all the elements that are included in reading facial expressions, which involve the eyes, eyebrows, lips, nose, and even the wrinkles around the eyes and mouth.

## PUPIL

There is practically no way to fake the movement of the pupils when reading facial expressions. The pupils of the eye contract and expand without any sort of control on the part of a person. Typically, the pupils will expand when a person is interested and contract when they're not.

## BLINKING MOTION

The eyes typically blink six to ten times per minute. When a person looks at something they find interesting, however, that blinking rate slows down drastically. It's therefore a great indicator when someone finds something interesting or attractive. It's often used as a sign of flirting or interest in a romantic setting. In an office or social setting, unblinking eyes could be a signal that a person is very interested in what you have to say and listening to you throughout.

## RAISING THE HEAD

Raising the head from a lowered position is a sign of captured interest. Think of a student who's looking down during an exam who suddenly raises their head when they hear something important. This is the kind of movement that we are trying to describe in this situation.

## HEAD TILT

A head tilt usually starts from a normal position of the head and then juts out at an angle. This is what makes it different from the motion of raising your head from a lowered position. A head tilt also indicates interest, usually towards the person or activity where it happens to be tilted too. When combined with facial expressions like a narrowing of the eyebrows, it can be a sign of confusion, curiosity, questioning, or uncertainty. A head that's tilted backward may be a sign of suspicion.

Of course, let's not forget the typical head gestures that mean practically the same for everyone. These are:

## NODDING

Usually signifies agreement.

### SHAKING THE HEAD

Usually signifies disagreement.

What's important about these gestures is that people are often conscious of doing this. Hence, it can be easily controlled by them, depending on the situation. Some can stop the motion entirely while others turn it into very subtle gestures so that it would be very difficult to notice.

## HANDS, ARMS, AND GESTURES

### SHRUG

A shrug is composed of multiple gestures which include exposed palms, hunched shoulders, and raised brows. It's a universal sign that indicates a lack of knowledge or uncertainty over a particular activity. It can often be translated as a sign that the other person doesn't know what you're saying or doesn't understand what you're trying to convey.

### CLENCHED HANDS

Clenched hands are a sign of repression. You're trying to prevent the burst of emotions like anger or frustration. It's a self-containment mechanism often used by people who don't want to do or say something out of order. In some cases, you can read this gesture as a sign that someone has a closed mind on what you're trying to say. In the alternative, open and relaxed hands are a sign of comfort and show a positive attitude with a mind welcome to new ideas.

## HAND WRINGING

This is often interpreted as a sign of anxiety or nervousness. Playing with something in your hands also has the same interpretation.

## HANDSHAKE

You have to be careful with handshakes as this can tell so much about a person and vice versa. I'm sure you've managed to have presumptions of people simply because of the way they shook your hand. The best handshake is often considered to be a firm, dry grip, that's quick but not too long. It shouldn't be too tight as to cause pain, but it should be strong enough to signify competence on the part of the person shaking their hand. My advice is you practice your handshake with another person to help you decide on the best pressure to use when greeting someone this way. Note though—not all cultures accept handshakes as a viable way of greeting others. For example, people in India or those who practice the Muslim faith do not approve of handshakes as a way of greeting between men and women.

## COVERING THE MOUTH

Doing this is often shown as a sign of repression, like a person wanted to say something but decided against it at the last minute. Some people use this gesture as a way to show thinking or a thought process.

# BODY POSTURE AND MOVEMENT

You've probably noticed that reading body language involves paying attention to different parts of the body all at once. Some gestures are centered in just one area, like the face, and therefore are slightly easier than others. Some gestures, however, are scattered all over the body, which means that different parts are moving all at once. This makes it tougher to do a reading, but you'll find that with practice, the whole thing becomes easier.

Body posture and movement is a big predictor of a person's thoughts and emotions. The general position of the chest, shoulders, legs, and so on will tell you if a person is aggressive, afraid, unsure, excited, and so on. Here are some of the typical changes in the body and what they indicate:

## A PUMPED-OUT CHEST IS A SIGN OF POWER AND DOMINANCE

Typically, when the chest is spread out, the shoulders are also stretched into a straight line, pushing the chest forward and making the person appear bigger. Combined with hands placed on the hips and this can be dubbed as the "Superman" pose which makes a person appear bigger and occupy more space. This is often seen as a sign of confidence and dominance. You'll notice many animals in the wild, when protecting their territory or trying to attract a mate, tend to make their bodies appear bigger so that they'll be easily noticed. Men and women do the same thing and often for the same reasons.

## TOUCHING THE CHEST CAN ALSO BE A SIGN OF SINCERITY

You'll notice how people do this when they're trying to apologize or communicate how bad they feel or their condolences to another person.

Scratching or touching the chest can also be a sign of discomfort.

## BREATHING

Breathing can tell you a lot about what a person feels. You've probably noticed this already, not just in other people but also in yourself. For example, you might hold your breath when excited or take short and shallow breaths when scared. Typically, deep and even breaths are indicative of relaxation, such as when you're sleeping or when you're sitting down watching a relaxing movie. Excessive, shallow, or holding your breath, on the other hand, can be a sign of emotional turmoil. According to experts, mirroring a person's breathing pattern can also help forge a connection of mutual understanding between the two of you. Being able to match someone's breathing pattern essentially allows you to create a sense of normalcy in the situation, thereby pulling them into a sense of relaxation. Of course, this takes some skill to do, especially if the situation is nerve-wracking. At the very least, being able to identify nervous breathing patterns can help you adjust your stance to make the other person feel comfortable—all without a word said to each other.

## READING LIES IN PEOPLE

One of the most valuable skills when reading people is being able to tell when they're lying. Admit it—you've always wanted to know when someone is lying to you, and that's perfectly okay. Studies show that when lying, some people have specific "tells," such as scratching their nose or brushing their hair with their fingers. People who play poker often use these "tells" to see if they should match the other person's bet and whether it would be worth the trouble.

One thing I want to remind you of is that reading lies in a person is not an exact science. People's actions when lying can vary, which is why familiarity is important. The longer you know a person, the more accurate your prediction will be about the truthfulness of what they're saying.

So, that being the case, here are the typical signs of lying according to experts.

## UNDERSTANDING A BASELINE

One thing I want you to remember is that when reading body language, there's usually a "baseline" that allows you to start somewhere. A baseline is simply the "normal" way in which a person acts when around people. Hence, if a person is being truthful and confident in their surroundings, how exactly do they act? Knowing a person's baseline lets you know when they're acting out of character. Sure, you can walk into a room full of strangers and do a casual "read" of the room, but reading people close to you is often easier as you've known them for a longer period. You have a point of reference, to put it simply.

## HAND MOVEMENTS

People lying tend to use gestures, but they do it after speaking. Typically, you'd find people gesturing while talking because that is a natural part of the process. Their body is working with the mind in telling a story or conveying a message. In contrast, a person who is lying is focusing too much on making up the story that the body fails to catch up. Hence, they make up the lie first and then perform the gestures to emphasize their point. Also, take note that gestures of people who are lying often involve both hands as opposed to truthful people who only use one hand. This was noted after a 2015 study about people testifying in court cases.

## ITCHING AND FIDGETING

There's a popular belief that when a person lies, they tend to scratch their nose. This isn't true 100% of the time—but it does bear noting in many cases. It's fairly normal for people to have an itching sensation or fidget in their seat when they're uncomfortable; the body naturally looks for a way to distract itself. Also note that when lying, people are often nervous about what they're saying, which causes the autonomic nervous system to fluctuate, thus, creating that tingling sensation all over the body. It's a lot like the nerves you get when you sit close to someone you like during those younger days.

## Facial Expressions

Of course, let us not forget how the face itself can signify when someone is lying. The eyes in particular can tell you so much depending on when a person chooses to look at you and when they choose to look away. Looking too much or not looking at all can be indicative of lying. Some people prefer to meet your gaze when lying because they "think" this will impress upon you their sincerity. Non-experienced liars tend to look away when uttering a lie.

## Change in Complexion

This one's pretty obvious, as you read about it every day or see it as it happens every day. People blush, people become red, and people become pale depending on the circumstances. People tend to become pale when they're nervous or when they're afraid of something. When the skin turns a shade of red, however, that's indicative of anger or perhaps even excitement, like when a teenager typically blushes when sitting beside their crush.

## Sweat in the T Zone

This is something you have to watch out for when wondering if a person is lying to you or not. The T Zone covers the area of the nose and across the forehead and then down to your mouth. Sweating is fairly common in this area if a person is lying, especially if they're nervous about it.

## TONE OF VOICE

We're trying to focus on nonverbal communication here, but the tone of voice is still a strong indicator, even with the absence of the words themselves. High-pitched voices tend to come out of nervous people as the vocal cords tighten, making it hard to push out the particular words. There can also be a croak, a stutter, or some broken words coming out of a nervous individual. Some people clear their throat to help improve their speech, which is also indicative of nervousness. In contrast, a loud and booming voice can be a sign of confidence or anger, depending on the situation. A sudden change in the volume can also be defensive in people, especially when confronted with possible mistakes.

## THE MOUTH

Playing with the lips, such as rolling them back until they almost disappear, is another good indicator. It's typically a sign of lying by omission as people physically try to hold back a word or a thought by pulling in their lips. If it goes the other way, however, it can be a sign of resistance or when a person doesn't want to talk about something.

## THE WORDS THEMSELVES

Again, we're trying to focus on the nonverbal way of communicating, but I still want to cover all bases. After all, experienced liars can easily control their body language to match the situation. Hence, you still have to listen to the words themselves as they can indicate when a person is trying too hard to convince you of their truthfulness. Some common phrases used by liars include:

"Honestly…"

"Let me tell you the truth…"

"Uh…"

"Like…"

"Um…"

# Chapter 4:

# Users of Dark Psychology

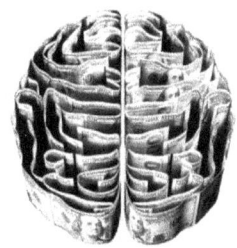

## WHO USES DARK PSYCHOLOGY THESE DAYS?

### ATTORNEYS

Many attorneys focus so attentively on winning their case that they turn to use techniques of dark manipulation to get the outcome they seek.

### THE SELFISH PEOPLE

Someone with a secret agenda that favors itself before anyone can return to those dark, deceptive tactics if the result is a win for them.

## POLITICIANS

To get the votes they need to get the people to vote in the way they want them, politicians are guilty of using dark methods of manipulation as a means of serving their purpose.

## LAWYERS

Some lawyers will stop at nothing if it means winning their case, even if it means they have to resort to shady tactics.

## SALESPEOPLE

Much like attorneys and politicians, specific salespeople may be so focused on doing nothing but selling that they have no shame in using deceptive techniques to convince a customer to do what they want.

## LEADERS

Not every leader is there to inspire, and some rely on manipulation to get us to meet their demands.

## PUBLIC SPEAKERS

Not all public speakers can be trusted, and there are some out there whowill resort to bribery if it means selling more goods to do so. Many speakers use dark strategies to heighten the audience's emotional state of realizing it leads to more products being sold at the back of the room.

These are just a few of the many instances of people out there who would turn to the more malevolent side of the continuum of human nature, and often for the benefit of no one else but their own.

# THE TRIAD OF DARK PSYCHOLOGY

Just when you felt the deceit was bad enough, an even darker side of psychology arrives here, known as the Dark Triad. The triad consists of three very distinct but interrelated forms of personality, namely narcissism, psychopathy, and Machiavellianism. Why is the Dark Triad, or the darker side of human psychology, called these three? It is because these three terms define the very tactics that some people resort to getting what they want-manipulation, persuasion, and deception. Yes, the term Dark Triad has a sinister ring to it, and it's a term that many psychologists and criminologists use as a defining predictor that signals an individual's criminal behavior. Let's look at the three personality characteristics that make up this trifecta more closely:

## NARCISSISM

The word comes from the Greek mythology of Narcissus, the hunter who fell in love with his reflection when he saw it in a pool of water where he drowned. He was so consumed by himself that he could not concentrate on anything else. Those with characteristics of narcissistic personality also show signs that include being boastful, greedy, and rude, caring more for themselves and nothing else. Also, narcissistic individuals lack empathy and are highly sensitive (one may even say hypersensitive) to any sort of criticism, since they cannot bear the incomplete or false thought.

## MACHIAVELLIANISM

This word comes from the famous diplomat and politician Niccolò Machiavelli who lived in Italy in the 16th century. Machiavelli became famous with the publication of his book, The Prince, in 1513. This publication has been interpreted as the recognition by Machiavelli of the deception and ruse that takes place in diplomacy. Those who tend to exhibit Machiavellianistic tendencies are often only concerned with their self-interest and are manipulative and duplicate. Some people lack both morals and conscience, so they're not into anything else but what's going to help them.

## PSYCHOPATHY

Antisocial behavior, manipulative, aggressive, violent, lack of guilt, or empathy are characteristics associated with a psychopathic character. Psychopathic and being a psychopath are two very different features, the latter generally associated with or explicitly associated with crime.

## THE MANIPULATOR

The term manipulative is likely to affect individuals of all social origins. The typical manipulator usually has a perverse psychological structure of the psychopathic type; he can appear as friendly or not, even as a victim. It seems that each one is more or less manipulative in the course of his life.

According to these definitions, different types of manipulators can be distinguished: those who use others without remorse, with a narcissistic goal of power, financial scam, or with malicious intent. They can rely on lies or seduction, even coercion by threat of force, or destabilize their victim by double oppression. Psychic manipulation can be one of the tools of certain forms of torture.

It can be behavior understood as deviant or perverse, a personality disorder whose causes go back to childhood or the manipulator's education, such as if his parents or educators have manipulated him. Psychologists are frequently confronted with manipulative behavior in systems such as family or socio-professional.

Mental manipulation could be a certain form of selfishness. Often the manipulator demands socially acceptable behavior from others without adapting themselves. He appropriates the ideas of another, conversely trying to make someone else take his responsibilities. The arguments of a manipulator always seem, at first glance, logical and moral. Usually, he uses pretexts such as the norm, the "good behavior" that must be observed in society or the group, knowing how to use the weaknesses of others, for example making them feel ridiculous, guilty, or hurt in their modesty, which places them in a mental situation favorable to manipulation.

## A SADIST

A professional sadist can so deliberately set these conditions up that it is impossible to prove that they were involved in the guilty party. What makes it far worse is that they will never be held responsible or feel any sort of regret for the harm they caused. People can also be hesitant to assume that the sadist's charming and likable personalities are behind the chaos. A sadist will attempt to harm someone else intentionally because they believe that doing so will benefit them. They may resort to such underhanded tactics if they feel envious or threatened by others or even if they perceive someone else as weaker and less likely to retaliate against them. In some instances, it might not be obvious why the sadist opted to conduct a victim attack. We don't often think-or want to believe-that the sadist might exist within our immediate circle of connections, but they do, and they could be your parents, siblings, extended family members, spouse, friends, and the people with whom you work.

## THE MANIPULATOR IN A RELATIONSHIP

One of the worst sinking feeling you might feel is knowing that all this time, your partner, the person you love and who supposedly loves you, turns out to be using you to their advantage. A partnership is supposed to be the one place we believe we can get the sincere inside support, love, dedication, and care we all yearn for. In return, to be wholeheartedly loved and respected. Sadly, there are those out there who have had their hearts broken because they know there's not just something dishonest about their partner, but they have manipulated their strings like a puppet all along.

We all have particular aspirations and romantic ideas of what we think love is due to the way in which love is portrayed in society through the films we watch, articles we read, and social media posts we scroll through almost every day. When we see on-screen jealousy, we believe it's a sign of intense love because the two people in the film are afraid to lose their loved one to another. The popular literature and Twilight movies lead us to believe that true love and relationships are about obsession. That love is an omnipresent emotion. That when there are two people in love, nothing else matters, and there are no boundaries. This romanticized notion blinds us to the fact that this isn't what life is at all, and that kind of love occurs only in movies and between the pages of books because they make for a good storyline. Such behavior is an indication of manipulation in real life. It is not love to be controlling, it is manipulation. It is not being passionate being obsessed, and it is manipulative.

On some level, we know that we should be able to recognize in a relationship the signs of an abusive partner. We know we can, but it is easier said than done. When we love, we prefer to blind ourselves to a fault with our mate. We are making excuses for the actions that should set off warning bells in our heads as we try to avoid facing the facts. We don't want our hearts to be broken that way, and we're trying to convince ourselves they aren't really like that at all. There is cause for concern when a relationship escalates from controlling to being purely abusive but being in a manipulative relationship can also be harmful and damaging.

Getting in a manipulative relationship can be as detrimental to you both physically and psychologically. Manipulative partners will try to dominate you, minimizing your freedom. They try to manipulate every decision you make, belittle you, and destroy your self-esteem so that you begin to doubt yourself and think you are the "lucky" one, and no one can possibly love you as much. They make you scared of losing this relationship and make you scared to enter into any future relationships because this experience has traumatized you from getting into another manipulative relationship. Being in a manipulative relationship will leave you with emotional wounds and scars that, if they ever do, will take a very, very long time to heal.

The more common signs you're in a manipulative relationship is when your partner continually pressures you to look or act in a way that they only approve of or decide who you can and can't spend your time with. The love and support that would come from genuine relationships is not something you will note when you're in a relationship with manipulators. Lying to try to manipulate you and the situation in their favor, when your partner is a manipulative person, is something that will be a regular occurrence in your relationship, and these are the signs to look out for:

- Lying to make you feel guilty about spending time with others—Because the manipulator needs to be in charge, they will try to cut you off as far as possible from your support network by trying to minimize the amount of time you spend with your family and friends.

- They lie and criticize— When you're with someone manipulative, every little thing you do is subject to criticism. The worst part of all this is that they lie so convincingly when they say they do it because "they love you" or "it's for your good". They'll continually criticize just about everything you're doing, the longer you remain in a relationship with them.

- You may be the most trustworthy and truthful person, but a manipulator will make you feel different. They are still individuals in their own right, as deeply in love as two people are, and all have the right to privacy.

- Manipulators may demand access to your passwords, social media accounts, and even more private information by spinning some tale about how they're "fearing" you might break their hearts by cheating on them.

- They're talking a lot about "protecting you," which, of course, is just another lie by the manipulator. They're not protecting you; they're not even thinking about it, because all they care about is their self-interest. Deep down, who wouldn't love the idea that there's somebody out there who loves them enough to protect them from the big evil world? That person exists, alas not with a manipulator. There's a natural desire to protect when you love someone and to keep them from feeling hurt.

- They provoke you with lies — Sometimes a manipulator might resort to provoking you into an argument by lying and exaggerating, blowing things out of proportion just because they know that when they do, and they push your buttons.

- Twisting lies with even more lies — Manipulators will spin lies almost as intricately as spinning their website. They will lie, twist those lies, and then twist those lies even more until you don't know what is real and what isn't. Twisting the truth and distorting them, tangling lies on top of more lies is the manipulator's favorite technique to confuse and frustrate you.

# Chapter 5:

# Behaviors Exhibited by Attackers

## EMOTIONAL INTELLIGENCE AND MANIPULATION

The term emotional intelligence was first invented in the 1960s and has become common over the years.

However, the concept behind the term has been around for decades. In simple terms, emotional intelligence is the ability of a person to recognize and understand emotions, then using this information to make decisions.

Like any other skill, emotional intelligence is a skill we can cultivate, sharpen, and enhance. It is important to note that although emotional intelligence is a good skill, one can use it either for good or bad.

Once a person understands the power of emotions, he or she can use it ethically or unethically.

The last thing that we want is having someone manipulating our emotions, whether it is a friend, colleague, or politician.

There are some ways through which a master manipulator can use emotional intelligence against you. Please note that not everyone who has the characteristics listed below and used the said skill has selfish intentions. Some people practice them with no intended harm. Nonetheless, having an increased awareness of these behaviors will empower you to deal with manipulators strategically and sharpen your intelligence quotient in the process.

## MANIPULATORS PLAY ON FEAR

The majority of manipulators will overemphasize specific points and exaggerate facts to make you scared and have you acting as they want. The way to identify this play is by looking out for statements that imply you are not strong or courageous enough or that if you miss out on a particular thing, you are a loser.

## MANIPULATORS DECEIVE

Everybody values honesty and transparency, thus, will want to avoid deceivers. Manipulators understand this concept and are very cunning when lying. They twist the facts or try to show you only the side of the story that benefits them. For instance, a work colleague can spread some unconfirmed rumor to gain an upper hand.

## MANIPULATORS TAKE ADVANTAGE OF YOUR HAPPINESS

Have you noticed that you are more likely to say yes to anything when you are happy or in a good mood? When we are happy, we tend to jump on opportunities that look good even before we think things through. Master manipulators have this knowledge, thus, will take advantage of the moods. To manage this emotional opportunity and avoid manipulation, work to improve awareness of your emotions, both positive and negative. strive to strike a balance between logic and emotions When making decisions.

## MANIPULATORS TAKE ADVANTAGE OF RECIPROCITY

Do you know that feeling you get when you owe someone a favor especially if they helped you at one point?

That feeling of debt makes one vulnerable. It is hard to say no to a manipulator if you owe them something.

Most of the manipulators will attempt to butter and flatter you with small favors then ask for a big one in return.

As much as giving brings more joy than receiving, it is more important to know your limits.

Do not be afraid to say no, even if you owe someone a favor.

## MANIPULATORS PUSH FOR A HOME-COURT ADVANTAGE

It is very easy to convince a person when you are in a familiar place. As such, a manipulator will push you towards meeting you in a place he or she is familiar with while you are not. Ownership gives power and comfort, thus, a place like home or the office will give the manipulator some authority. You will have to make requests for meeting in a neutral place where familiarity and ownership are diluted to disarm the manipulator.

## THE MANIPULATOR WILL ASK A LOT OF QUESTIONS

Naturally, it is easy to talk about oneself. Master manipulators know this; thus, they take advantage to ask some probing questions.

Their agendas are hidden but they seek to discover your weaknesses or other information they can hold against you.

Of course, it would be unfair for you to assume that everyone has wrong motives because there are a few people who genuinely seek to know you better. However, it is okay to question people, especially those who reveal nothing about themselves.

## THE MANIPULATOR WILL SPEAK QUICKLY

To manipulate you through your emotions, the manipulator will speak quickly and sometimes use jargon and special vocabulary.

This will give them an advantage because you will not have enough time to think. For you to counter this form of manipulation, do not feel afraid to ask for some time to process what the person said. Also, make a point of asking the person to repeat any unclear statements. To gain control of a conversation, repeat the points the other person makes in your own words, and let them sink in.

## THE DISPLAY OF NEGATIVE EMOTIONS

Some manipulators will use voice tones to control your emotions. The most commonly used tone and body language by manipulators are negative.

For instance, basketball coaches (they use manipulation for positive purposes) are masters at raising their voices and using strong body language to manipulate the emotions of the players. To avoid such manipulation, you should practice pausing. It involves taking a break from the conversation or situation and having some time to think before reacting. You may walk away for some minutes to get a grip on your own emotions.

## MANIPULATORS LIMIT YOUR TIME TO ACT

Every manipulator wants to win. They may do this by ensuring that you do not have enough time to think. For instance, an individual may force you to make a serious decision in an unreasonably limited amount of time.

He or she will try to steer your thoughts to their advantage. You will not have enough time to weigh the consequences. To avoid a situation where you give in without thought, do not be in a rush to submit. Ensure that the demand is reasonable. Take the pause, ask for some time, and if the person does not allow you to think, walk away. You will be happier looking for whatever you need elsewhere.

## THE SILENT TREATMENT

To avoid being a victim of manipulation through silent treatment, give people deadlines, and do not allow them to intimidate you.

For instance, after attempting to communicate to a reasonable degree, let go of the matter and let the other person reach out.

Manipulators will work to increase their emotional awareness to have an upper hand on others. A large number of people are learning how to be emotionally intelligent.

# CHARACTERISTICS OF MANIPULATORS

## USE OF LANGUAGE

We have shown how powerful language can bea prime tool of persuasion. There is more to the manipulative controller though, than mere words. They will use tactics that mislead and unbalance their target's inner thoughts. We now understand that through language, they will:

Use mistruths to mislead and confuse their target's normal thinking pattern.

Force their target to decide the speed, so they don't have time to analyze and think.

Overwhelmingly talk to their target, making them feel small.

Criticize their target's judgment so they begin to lose their self-esteem.

Raise the tone of their voice and not be afraid to use aggressive body language.

Ignore their target's needs, as they are only interested in getting what they want and at any cost.

## INVASION OF PERSONAL SPACE

Most of us set boundaries around ourselves without realizing we are doing so. It is a kind of unspoken rule to protect our own private space, such as not sitting so close that you are touching another person, especially a stranger. A manipulative character cares nothing about overstepping such boundaries. Whether this is because they do not understand, or they do not care is unclear. Initially, they are unlikely to invade their target's personal space. They will seek to build up a good rapport first. This shows that they do understand boundaries because once they gain the confidence of their target, they will then ignore them.

## FODDER FOR THOUGHT

Manipulators tend to be very egocentric, with limited social skills. Their only concern is for themselves. Everything they do in life will be concerning how it affects them, not how their actions affect others. Does this mean that they have a psychopathic disorder?

## CREATING RIVALRY

Another tactic of the controlling manipulator is backstabbing. They may tell you how great a person you are to your face, making themselves look good. Behind your back, they are busy spreading malicious gossip and untruths about you. This is a classic trait of a controlling manipulator as it creates a rivalry between people. Then, they can pick sides that will make them look favorable, particularly to their target. It can act as the first stage of getting close to their target. Once bonded, they can start to build up trust, making it easier to manipulate the target in the future. If you recognize a backstabber, keep them at a distance. Their agenda is selfish, so it is better not to let them into your personal life. There is no point treating them as they treat you as revenge. It will turn out to be exhausting playing them at their own game. If they know that you are onto them, they may attempt to lure you back with praise, remember that it is false.

## DOMINEERING PERSONALITY

It is unlikely that a manipulative person will outwardly show any form of weakness. An important part of their facade is to show conviction about their views. They seek to impress, believing they are right about everything. Almost to the point that if they realize they are wrong, they will still argue that they are right. On a one-to-one level, that invariably means that your position is always wrong.

## PASSIVE AGGRESSIVE BEHAVIOR

A common trait of many hard-core manipulators is passive-aggressive behavior. Because they prefer to be popular, they do not wish to be seen as doing anything wrong. Not that a manipulator would ever admit to doing anything wrong. They are experts with facial expressions that are meant to dominate and intimidate. This may include; knitting eyebrows, grinding teeth, and rolling eyes. It may also include noises such as tutting and grunting sounds.

## MOODY BLUES

What of the emotional stability of the manipulator? Is it that which makes them behave the way they do? Do they even know what happiness is? The answer to that is most definitely yes, at least to the latter.

Happiness is a tool used initially to help them manipulate, as a happy target is more likely to comply. This, in itself, makes the manipulator happy, or at least in a sense of what they consider happiness. But their joyfulness is a perverted model of what most others consider happiness to be. Their happiness is often built on the foundations of another's misery.

## ACCUSING YOUR RIVAL OF WHAT HE IS BLAMING YOU FOR

This is often referred to as the act of pointing to another person's wrongdoing. When enduring an onslaught and experiencing difficulty regarding safeguarding themselves, manipulators tend to reverse the situation. They blame their rivals for committing the exact things that they are being blamed for. *"You state that I don't love you! I think it is you who does not cherish me!"*

## APPEALING TO POWER

Numerous individuals are in wonderment of those in power or authority, or those who have status. What's more intriguing is that there are various images to which individuals experience extraordinary dedication. Remember, those who are easily manipulated admire those who are in power. Moreover, those who are in power are aware of their ability to control others by never criticizing them. Instead, they use complex misleading tactics to maneuver their thoughts and alter their decision-making process.

## APPEALING TO ENCOUNTER

Nevertheless, this appeal to experience provides them with an image of someone capable; this may be used to attack their opponent's lack of experience, even though they have limited experiences. You can easily identify this manipulation tactic at times when someone is trying to distort their capabilities about a particular subject.

## APPEALING TO FEAR

People have fears. The unscrupulous manipulators realize a reality that individuals will, in general, respond crudely when any of these feelings of dread are enacted. Subsequently, they speak to themselves as being able to ensure individuals against these dangers, even when they are not capable of doing so. This is the same for when we talked about giving the target a glimpse of how their most desired outcome is achievable, without really providing it to them. Nonetheless, some politicians and legislators frequently utilize this methodology to ensure that individuals line up behind administrative experts and do what the legislature – that is, the government officials – need.

## APPEALING TO SYMPATHY

Manipulators can depict themselves and their circumstances to the public to make them feel frustrated about their current situation.

Utilization of this ploy empowers the manipulator to gain consideration from those individuals who may be going through the same thing. Nevertheless, appealing to sympathy is a tactic that most politicians would use to redirect the attention of the public to matters that do not affect their demise.

## APPEALING TO WELL-KNOWN INTERESTS

Manipulators and tricksters are always mindful as to how they introduce themselves as persons who possess the right qualities and perspectives among the group of spectators, particularly, the sacred beliefs of the crowd. Everybody has a few partialities, and a great many people feel contempt toward a person or thing. Expert manipulators tend to stir up contempt and prejudices among the crowd.

## APPEALING TO CONFIDENCE

This technique is firmly identified with the past points; yet it stresses what appears to have breezed through the trial of time. Individuals are regularly oppressed by the social traditions and standards of their way of life, just as social conventions. What is conventional to most tend to appear as if it is the correct decision. It is important to note that manipulators infer how they regard sacred ideologies and beliefs that the group of spectators are familiar with. These individuals suggest that their enemy aims to obliterate the customs, as well as social conventions. Moreover, they do not stress over whether or not these conventions hurt guiltless individuals. They make the presence of being autonomous in the crowd's perspective; yet it would typically be the exact opposite. There is a realization that people are generally suspicious of the individuals who conflict with present social standards and built up conventions. They realize enough to stay away from them. As a result, there is a kind of restriction on how social traditions are unwittingly and carelessly bound.

## BEGGING THE INQUIRY

One simple approach to demonstrate a point is to accept it in any case. Think about this model:

"Well, what type of government do you want, a government by liberal do-gooders that can shell out your hard-earned dollars or a government controlled by business minds that know how to live within a strict budget and generate jobs that put people to work?"

One minor departure from this error has been classified as "question-begging epithets," the utilization of expressions is a prejudgment of an issue by how it is allowed. For instance, "Shall we defend freedom and democracy or cave into terrorism and tyranny?" Through the inquiry along these lines, we abstain from discussing awkward inquiries like: "Yet, would we say we are truly propelling human opportunity? Are we truly democratic or simply expanding our capacity, our control, our predominance, our access to foreign markets?" Keep in mind that these are statements individuals utilize when bringing about the truth concerning an issue. There is the regular choosing of statements that surmise the accuracy of the situation on a particular issue.

## CREATING A FALSE DILEMMA

A genuine problem happens when we are compelled to pick between two similarly unsuitable choices. A false dilemma happens when we are convinced that we have just two, similarly inadmissible decisions, when we truly have multiple potential outcomes accessible to us. Think about the accompanying case: *"Either we will lose the war on terrorism, or we should surrender a portion of our traditional freedoms and rights."*

Individuals are frequently prepared to acknowledge a false dilemma since few are agreeable with the complex qualifications. Clearing absolutes is a part of their manipulative tactics. There is a need to have clear and basic decisions.

## HEDGING WHAT YOU STATE

Manipulators frequently hole up behind words, declining to submit themselves or give straightforward replies or answers. This enables them to withdraw in times of need. Whenever they are found forgetting data significant to the current situation, they would think of some other reason for not being able to come up with said information. At the end of the day, when forced, they may be able to give in; however, to be an excellent manipulator, you should renege on your missteps, conceal your mistakes, and gatekeep what you state at whatever point conceivable.

## OVERSIMPLIFYING THE ISSUE

Since most people are uncomfortable at comprehending profound or unobtrusive contentions, some are fond of oversimplifying the issue to further their potential benefit. *"I couldn't care less what the measurements inform us concerning the purported abuse of detainees; the main problem is whether we will be tough on crime. Spare your compassion toward the criminals' victims, not for the actual criminals."* The reality being overlooked is that the maltreatment of criminals is a crime in itself. Tragically, individuals with an over-simple mindset could not care less about criminal conduct that victimizes criminals.

## RAISING ONLY COMPLAINTS

Your adversary is giving valid justifications to acknowledge a contention; however, the truth of the matter is that your mind's made up and nothing can change it. Gifted manipulators would react with objection after objection. As their rivals answer one protest after another, they would proceed again to object and object. The implicit mentality of the manipulator is that *"regardless of what my rival says, I will continue to object because nothing else will convince me otherwise."*

## REWRITING HISTORY

The most noticeably awful acts and outrages tend to vanish from chronicled accounts while false dreams can be made to become facts. This phenomenon is often observed with Patriotic History. The composition of a contorted type of history is supported by the adoration of the nation and is regularly defended by the charge of antagonism. The truth of the matter is that our mind is persistently attempting to re-portray occasions of the past to absolve itself and denounce its spoilers. Chronicled composing frequently goes with the same pattern, particularly in the composition of reading material for schools. In this way, in recounting an anecdote about what has happened, those who perform manipulative tactics do not hesitate to contort the past in the manners in which they accept they can pull off. As usual, the manipulator is prepared with self-justifying excuses.

## SHIFTING THE BURDEN OF PROOF

This act alludes to when an individual should demonstrate some of his declarations. A good example would be the instance that happened inside a court. The examiner possesses the obligation to prove guilt past distrust. Furthermore, the defense should not claim the responsibility of having to prove innocence. Those who are capable of manipulating others do not need to assume the weight of evidence for what they attest to. Along these lines, they harness the right tool in shifting the burden of proof to their rivals.

## TALKING IN VAGUE GENERALITIES AND STATEMENTS

It is difficult to refute individuals when they cannot be bound. So, as opposed to concentrating on specifics, those who are capable of manipulating others tend to speak in the most unclear phrases that they can pull off. We have already talked about how certain statements and generalities can put another person in a daze, which makes it easier for them to be manipulated. This misrepresentation is well known for politicians. For instance, ***"Overlook what the cowardly liberals say. It's the right time to be tough, to be hard on criminals, to punish terrorists, and be tough on those who disparage our nation."*** Manipulators ensure they do not utilize particulars that may make individuals question what they are doing in the first place.

## TELLING ENORMOUS FALSEHOODS AND BIG LIES

The majority of the people are liars, even about the little things; yet there is still a reluctance to say things other than the truth. In any case, these individuals realize that if you insist on a lit long enough, numerous individuals will trust you – particularly, on the off chance that you have the tools of mass media to broadcast a particular lie.

Every gifted manipulator is centered around what you can get individuals to accept, not on what is valid or false. They realize that the human personality does not normally look for reality; it looks for solace, security, individual affirmation, and personal stake.

Individuals regularly would prefer not to know the reality, particularly, certainties that are agonizing, that uncover their logical inconsistencies and irregularities, and that uncover what they hate about themselves or even their nation.

Some so many manipulators are exceptionally gifted in telling huge lies and, in this manner, causing those lies to appear valid.

## INTIMIDATION

One aspect of manipulation, often used as a last resort, is intimidation and bullying. When everything else has failed, they begin to use threats to get their way. Some though, may use intimidation from the onset. It may be a source of authority. For example, let's take the role of a manipulative boss. You have requested a day off. They don't want to allow your request but have no choice, it is your right. This type of person would want their pound of flesh first. They will set goals for you to reach so it will delay or cancel your request, such as moving project deadlines forward. This way they have their little victory over you.

## THE ASSET OF LISTENING

Listening can be perhaps the most important persuasive tactic you have in your tool kit. Listening to your prospect will give you most of the information you need for a successful persuasive conversation. By listening and paying careful attention to the words and body language, your prospect is communicating and by listening carefully for the words they don't say, you'll be able to discern most of what you need.

## THE FAVOR OF O SMILE

Your ability to smile is one of the most powerful tools to influence. This is true of influencing yourself or others. We've learned over thousands of years that the smile is a sign of happiness and friendship, so the smile helps to lower our defenses. When individuals smile, dozens of influential processes happen automatically.

## GHOSTING YOU

Guys do this a lot, even if it is something as simple as ghosting you, because it trains you to not get used to hearing from him at certain times, and you always have to reach out to see how he is doing and checking to see if he remembers the date that he set for you. They use their profession or their education to delay you finding out the truth or make you feel like they're always the right one.

## DEMONIZE YOUR REACTIONS

They tend to demonize your reactions because anytime someone that is manipulating you and they don't want you to be able to express yourself or control the situation, they will make you feel like you are the bad guy for reacting the way that you did to the situation. They will flip the script on you because you didn't agree with their actions.

You might tell him, "Hey, babe, I don't know why you just liked this girl's picture on Instagram. I thought that we agreed that you won't do this. You show me their stuff. It makes me feel embarrassed that my boy is liking the girl's photos and commenting on rubbish on Instagram, and it makes me feel insecure because you are my boyfriend". Then he will say something like, "you are so insecure, it's just Instagram, I can't believe that you are seriously talking to me about a comment that I wrote to a girl. First of all, I don't even know her, and she looks nice. Other guys are commenting on her photos, but why do you care because I'm with you". So, they demonize you and make you feel like the way you feel is not accounted for. They invalidate the way you feel because he doesn't know that girl, and he may even be trying to get to know her.

## **USING PITY**

One of the greatest forms of manipulation is by using pity. Getting pity out of anybody will guilt-trip them, so because they feel bad for you, they will do what you say, hear you out and whatever trash you want to slip.

For instance, if you say, "I just realized that when we were at the get-together, you didn't want to hang out with me. You were just doing your own thing. I don't know everybody there, I felt alone, and I understand that you know everybody, but I didn't feel included." Then he will say something like, "Honey, I'm sorry that you didn't feel included. However, what do you expect me to do, all the people were people that I grew up with. So, I'm sorry that I wasn't holding your hand the entire time, but I did introduce you to some people. You know that I wouldn't do that to you. You know that I am not like that. I was just caught up. Plus, I saw one of my girlfriends from high school and we just started talking. Come on, if you know me, you know that I wouldn't do something like that. I am not like that."

## IT MAKES YOU FEEL GUILTY, AND YOU DON'T KNOW WHY

A master of manipulation consistently goes to victimization. They likely have a "wild card trauma," that is, some problematic episodes in their life that they always expose as a justification for what they do incorrectly.

If, for example, you complain to them for their lack of consideration, they respond by saying something like "you get angry because I am not considerate, but I had to put up with a father who abandoned me when I was three years old." Thus, they disarm you with their traumas. Who will be so insensitive as to complain to someone who has such a past? This is their game.

## IT THREATENS YOU WITH SUBTLETY

Threatening indirectly is one of the most recurrent tactics among manipulators. They have used it and continue to use it from the great leaders to the small domestic tyrants, passing through seasoned publicists. This tactic consists of anticipating the worst possible outcome as a consequence of any of your behaviors.

"If you keep eating that way, in 6 months, you will be like a whale." They don't want you to eat, and they probably have no arguments to certify what they say, they just want you not to. Maybe they are bothered by how happy you are when you eat ice cream, or they think you spend too much money on food. They do not openly tell you what they believe, but merely announce a hecatomb.

## DISQUALIFY WHAT YOU DO THROUGH SARCASM

If there's one thing a master manipulator hates, it's direct communication. "They don't name you a dog, but they offer you a bone," goes the famous saying. They often use sarcasm to ridicule you or downplay the value of your thoughts, feelings, or actions. The manipulator wants others to feel insecure and inferior.

An example of this is when they send you a seemingly friendly message, but which contains quite aggressive content: "Maybe if you read a little more, you could have more select friends." Translated means: "You are an uneducated person, and that's why your friends are poor devils."

Sometimes, the manipulator's victim comes to believe that these kinds of insights are ways to help him be better. Nothing is falser. When someone wants to help another, use direct and honest communication. Also, it does not disqualify you but instead gives you a concrete contribution.

## HE IS ALMOST ALWAYS CHARMING

Typical handlers know that "the horse is stroked to mount it." They usually start their job by looking cute and enjoyable. They fill you with compliments and show signs of exquisite tastes, super-entertaining conversation, and high "sensitivity" to your expectations.

## SET YOURSELF THE JUDGE OF YOUR LIFE

Without knowing how suddenly the master of manipulation becomes a "spiritual guide" for your life. They are incredibly adept at telling others how they should live, even if they do not put into practice all that they proclaim.

They give you advice or expose your great philosophical sayings. They tell you what to do, bit by bit. If it doesn't work out, they blame you. He told you what to do, dare if you did not follow precisely the instructions that he so generously offered you.

# Conclusion

There has been lots of discussion about dark psychology, how and in which situations it is practiced most commonly and what the factors hidden behind it are. This is also considered to be a dark side of human nature, which is seldom exposed. Every human being, no matter how nice and positive they are, are always going to be evil in someone else's eyes. For the person whom you made suffer, you are evil, even if you deny it. Every person must evaluate him or herself and see if any of the hazardous or negative elements are found in them. You have to keep fighting your dark side so that it does not take control over you completely. Once you know to keep off that side, you will be able to identify it in others as well and can prevent yourself from falling prey to it. One must be aware of its indications and related signs so that people who have the qualities of dark psychology can be avoided. If you have fallen prey to dark psychology, then there is a chance for you to regain normality by assessing and evaluating yourself or by seeking medical advice.

Remember that deception is not always practiced on other people. We can often self-deceive to preserve our self-esteem. Telling ourselves that we can achieve certain goals when all the evidence points to the fact that we can't, is a healthy form of deception, but self-deception can lead to serious delusions.

Whatever happens in the novice stages of your path to becoming a master of manipulation and persuasion, you must remember your end goal. Ask yourself in the beginning why you want to do this and keep coming back to that when it gets hard. Never give up; you are to master these skills.

I hope that through this book, you have realized that brainwashing, manipulation, and persuasion depends greatly on an authoritative command of words. You might be able to list twenty manipulation techniques from memory; you may be able to get someone with little psychic resistance to go with your ideas.

You may have gotten to the end of the book — and you may have all the knowledge necessary to manipulate people — but you are just beginning when it comes to putting this all into practice.

Also, remember manipulation is classified into positive and negative (Egocentric and Malicious). The study shows how toavoid negative manipulators and try as hard as possible to stay in your lane. Work on the positive aspect of manipulation to help yourself and help others — best of luck!

www.ingramcontent.com/pod-product-compliance
Lightning Source LLC
Chambersburg PA
CBHW071124030426
42336CB00013BA/2197